The Heart's Traffic

THE HEART'S TRAFFIC

a novel in poems

✤

Ching-In Chen

ARKTOI BOOKS | LOS ANGELES, CALIFORNIA

Book design by Mark E. Cull
Author photograph by Teri Elam

ISBN: 978-0-9800407-2-2
Library of Congress Catalog Card Number: 2008934879

Arktoi Books is an imprint of Red Hen Press
First Edition

Printed in Canada

ACKNOWLEDGEMENTS

Eloise Klein Healy for helping me put all the stones in place and for building a community I can belong to. Nickole Brown; and Mark E. Cull, Kate Gale, and Red Hen Press for helping me push my words into the world.

Those who were the first to teach me well—Maiana Minahal, who first introduced me to the poetic forms of poets of color; Suheir Hammad, who wouldn't let me quit; Madeleine Lim, who expected the highest in me; Truong Tran, for encouraging my play on the page; Ruth Forman, for teaching me with fierce grace; Arthur Sze, who opened up a path towards the poetic sequence; liz gonzález, for daring me to open up to the persona poem; and Cornelius Eady, who gave me permission to hope.

Those who invested the time to read my manuscript with great care and love—James Autio, Ann Hostetler, Tamiko Beyer, Vanessa Huang, Soham Patel, Juan Felipe Herrera, Chris Abani, Liz Bradfield, and the ALAG poets.

Sylvia La for the beautiful art gracing my cover. Guang Li Zhang for the painting of the sparrow.

Sarah Gambito, Joseph O. Legaspi, Oliver de la Paz, Vikas Menon and the Kundiman family; Elmaz Abinader, Diem Jones and the VONA family; R. Erica Doyle, Naomi Jackson and the fierce women of Tongues Afire—these communities kept me writing when I was ready to put down my pen.

Marilyn Nelson and Tonya Hegamin of Soul Mountain Retreat and Alice Green and Charles Touhey of Paden Institute—for the space to let go and to dip deeply.

The first Mangos With Chili crew—Leah Lakshmi Piepzna-Samarasinha and Maria Cristina Rangel, aka Miss Cherry Galette (the best boss ladies in the world!); and Thomas Andre Bardwell, Kay Barrett, Ignacio Rivera, Dulani, and Victor Tobar—for letting me test-run Xiaomei on the road from city to city and loving her on repeat.

To all who walked the path with me at different points and let me know I wasn't alone—and especially, Aimee Lee, my opposite twin; Marlon Unas Esguerra, the muskrat who transmitted the bones of many poems; Sham-e-Ali Al-Jamil, self-care buddy extraordinaire; Rona Luo; R. A. Villanueva; Bryan Thao Worra; Matthew Olzmann; Phayvanh Luekhamhan; Neil Aitken; and Barbara Jane Reyes.

Previously Appeared

Grateful acknowledgement is made to the editors of the publications in which versions of poems from this book first appeared:

Tea Party: "fob";
Fifth Wednesday Journal: "Cool Li?: a riddle?";
OCHO: "[3. Girl.]," "Fifth Day of Silence," "Xiaomei's First Heartbreak," "Lightning Love: a Zuihitsu";
Poemeleon: "Cowrie: a riddle," "Fighting Over Stars," "Xiaomei's Father, Again," and "The True Tale of Xiaomei. "

Also, a thank you to those involved in transforming "The Geisha Author Interviews" into a living and breathing poem on the stage in the Playworks festival.

For my family—the ones I've received and the ones I've chosen

CONTENTS

IV. Onion Dreams

—ⵡ—

—ⵡ—

—ⵡ—

—ⵡ—

—ɯ—

The Heart's Traffic

I

Makeshift Family Myth

Cooled Ghee: *a riddle*

Long ago, two temporary fathers lived in an unmentionable land far from home. Under the tear-dry sun, the thin father from the North sang the songs passed down from his youth in his clear voice. The tall father from the South collected the elements of water, sand, dirt, and green for his stories with no end, no matter how wide the field grew in the night while they mumbled to their lost families. When the almond-colored father bent his waist to the rhythm in the field, his legs grew into tree trunks. The barktree father wished for the old morning smell buried in the luggage that fell over the ribcage of the boat which brought them. But the fathers had no other relatives or friends there, and eventually they grew weary of each other. One day, the father with the wide-brim hat asked the other: "Brother, do you ever wish we had a mother to lie down with us on our mat in the darkness?" The cloth-wrapped father kept his face still. But his voice swallowed lakes, and he bid the hero of his tale to slip off the ship's hull into the salt water, and that was the end of the never-ending story. Year by year, the lights went out. The two fathers ground their shoulders to the bottom of the dirt field, their sweat libations to free themselves of their contract. The song and story lived in the cough and stir of the chest, the bend of the waist, the pump of the leg, but neither heard the other. Arriving at the end of their contract, the fathers discovered unexpected fees and circumstances. Instead of Eastern passage, each father received new relatives on the same hot day.   The father who ate bamboo asked the father with the drum: "Do we even remember how to push our voices into the morning?" They'd left the sounds fluttering between them in the back of their histories where their families stayed. The new family opened their mouths, and old home greetings rained from the sky.

II

Inventing the Island

XIAOMEI'S FIRST HEARTBREAK

Gone the clanging midnight door, perpetual raised voice.
Xiaomei wakes in the dew, the traffic of her heart missing.

Her father did not say goodbye. Or he visited her, a stealth-owl dream.

                                                 Either way, her memory
does not appear at the short wooden door or trail her through the full streets like
the older boys in the neighborhood.

Her mother does not cry, but continues.

Every morning,
gruel
      pickle

             quick to schoolbag
                       onto the noise of street.
                       He disappeared into the black hole of America,
                an odd place with beer-drinking, restaurant-opening
                aunties and cousins who like cereal.

             No letter arrives.

Xiaomei & Sparrow

a renga

wind figure squatting
sharp-eyed laughing braids behind
papaya milk stand

from tied black river hair, down
the soft sun where your voice lives

secret secret press
against teasing mouth of fruit,
mountain come undone

and you across the river
of mud-eyed market people

each body each bo-
dy to come closer, friend or
flight, a smiling hand

first first between us you first
lift the branch of arm greeting

a bolt a laugh sun
breaking open papaya
amber scoop black seeds

you offer golden laugh sweet
i eat skin and spit out bone

warm descends wakes moon
stalls unravel into carts
peddle oyster cake

i you i hand and hand we
ask again and again we

hurry each body
past the stinking litter street
late oh late scurry

we break apart break apart
new friend filling into dream

dream sizzle fry salt
morning market smell for two
hungry girls gather

yes sister yes to shared night-
secret of sugarcane juice

and red-bean riddle.

COWRIE: *a riddle*

From a father of infrequent gifts,
the smooth cream orb tucked in the mouth of her schoolbag.

What becomes treasure?

Do they keep with you,
transactions which circle behind the back,
the spirit of what you have let unravel,
those hours lived in simple houses,
when family meant a layer between the breathing and the gentle dead?

In her questioning hand,
Xiaomei holds her father's final riddle
before his body transforms into a new American man.

XIAOMEI'S SONG

While pouring congee into bowls:
    papaya
    papaya
    papaya
    papaya

Laden with a precious list:
    fresh leaf from Ma Chen
    unwrapped rice clump
    Auntie Hsu's 2 bitter melons
    4 blocks of tofu from Yuen Yuen's

At the appointed time:
    by the missing stand
    of the nighttime
    underwear vendor

Where is Sparrow?
    Missing
    Missing
    Missing!
    Little girl hurtling down the street, lightning bolt!

KNOTS

a double sestina

Dear Sparrow,
let's meet
at the tree
in the school-
yard, day
after next.
Keep this
secret.
We
can leave
notes
too. Xiaomei

They build a nest,
Sparrow & Xiaomei,
using dank
dirt & knots
behind school
where they leave
gifts at the tree
hidden by weeds
when they can't meet.
They like secrets,
especially Sparrow,
her envelopes thick.

X, leaving
you this
blue spool
of thread. Sparrow
Note
contains secret
time of day
to meet.
Xiaomei
(when
sun kisses the next
maple tree)

Secret
maple tree,
thick knots
knees
grip, sallow
bark to weave.
Sparrow soon
teaches Xiaomei
how to do this,
dangling feet
under leaves
each day.

S, we
shared the best day
plucking narrow
shirt sleeves
from the next
market-day mat.
I keep all your notes,
save this
one for the tree.

Invented greeting
during school—
left hand next
to seat,
means left
path for Xiaomei,
right for Sparrow
until reaching the tree.
Only certain days

Xiaomei
(a secret
after school)

Xiaomei,
note
what we leave
now. We
think it's secret.
But these
new
markings in the dirt?
After school,
tree
meet.
Sparrow

I saved you some tea
you like, buried next
to the tree we
swallowed
sweets
that day.
Brewing season
means time for kites,
Sparrow.
Tomorrow after school,
let's do this
exchange before we leave.

Every school's
dangerous secret,
Xiaomei,
buried in rings of the tree.
Every uncovering, this
should be noted
down for when we meet
next.

do we need this.
Other times, we
just pass notes.

This is
Sparrow's new
secret—
meet
where
the tea
leaves
and spoons
nap
at the close of the day,
sugar
in the room next.

Each day
the girls leave,
dream meeting
again. What adventure this
time, asks Xiaomei?
This new school
of dreams wild,
helmed by Sparrow,
always ready. The next
game, detailed in notes,
which tree
deemed secret.

Ritual, hidden notes,
times we
became saltlines. This
during days
when only lonely tree
winked at Sparrow,
cup of tea for Xiaomei.
Leaves

Then, leave
for Sparrow
for the day
when we. . . .

Sparrow, you I will always meet
by tree embracing school
day after next,
glorious secret
we never fully leave
in notes. Xiaomei

hiding secrets,
the next
path through school
until sunset when we meet.

FIGHTING OVER STARS

Xiaomei and Sparrow, two girls on the horizon
      between burning sun and the pitchsong of dark blood,
    hover in hard breath,
        weaving thick air sticky as new-year sweet rice.

They brood over the birthing stars, prick each other's bright eye.

They love with clutched fingers,
hate each other like new blood.

Not yet angry, the evening screeches.

One girl casually hazards a guess, shoots the opening volley.
The other guards the door of her mouth.

The first girl repeats.
The other counters,

                        her voice spilling disagreement.
The first   love like grains of uncooked rice,
      and the other   love like vagabond train robbers

          dissolving into the chirping or descending night.

SOME SAY

Some say a little girl fell into the lake that night and nobody's seen her since.

Some say it was the black sky she ran to, a girl in love with midnight.

Some say if only.

Some say the lake, lonely and hungry, set a trap for winged creatures and the little girl was too lovely for her own good.

Some say they've sighted a little figurine, pale as a shirt washed too many times, drifting in lonely places.

Some say when little girls pass, they transform into useful things like lanterns greeting the weary farmers enticed by the rippling lake.

Some say there are no such things.

Some say the lake digests all her daughters and births fireflies.

No one says, I will miss her my whole-long life. I will carve a door in my dream, an entrance that belongs only to her so I can tell her again and again how I wish we never fought over the stars the night she fell out of my life.

Dear S,

There is something else you did not know.
I am a blue-ribbed oyster and lonely.
You were the first to go
to the edge
and I don't know if I can pardon you
if you never come back.

—Xiaomei

III

The Still Migrating Body

Gruel, Tea: *a riddle*

A room full of fathers birth
maggots which boil
into a sticky bag of
soup. Some sons
learned to suckle
too tightly, their
incandescent greed
dropping into the pot.
Others memorized
the recipe of how to
survive without.

Will follow you for 1,000
miles without breaking sweat,
desires neither to be fed or
clothed, fears neither guns nor
soldiers, can kiss the bruising
sun or coax a lullaby from the
dying mother.

Wars have been lit in its name.

Xiaomei's Father, Again

Here, in the song between two still bodies, is a new man she does not recognize.

Black Reebok sneakers. Faded blue jeans streaked with sweat. Plaid shirt stuffed hastily into the waistband. Over this, an olivegreen coat thick as snow.

Xiaomei's father, an ocean.

Xiaomei grasps her mother's hand
tightly, wishes she were
home, and swallows her nagging
voice.

THE NEW WORLD

a sestina

I cannot remember
the thunder grandfather
masquerading as my adult.
We did not place our belongings in the refrigerator.
Our home lived in the screen of a television
filling the room more than our original smiles.

There was a day we filled the one suitcase with grainy smiles
we remembered
when disembarking like the families on television,
minus the grandfather
we left begging at the altar of an empty refrigerator.
Our legacy's last remaining adult

is always become the adult
who smiles
as he unplugs the lonely pea-green refrigerator
and sweeps the last room of all its dust. Will we remember
again each grandfather?
Each avenue bears a display window, encased television.

There are no signs of the missing on television.
When you become an adult,
my mother explained, we can return to visit grandfather.
She smiled,
but I distrusted and now I do not remember.
My new family fills the refrigerator

now with new treasure. Steel refrigerator
and large-screen color television,
warm and snug in the corners. When I remember,
I will be a grown adult
with shiny smiles
searching for Grandfather.

Grandfather,
we have stocked the refrigerator
in honor of your smiles.
This legend of television
encourages each adult
to dis-remember

her own grandfather.
In each land, there is a refrigerator
filled to the brim with smiles.

FATHER'S SONG

A worn boot. Discarded shirt. The eye of a button. Whiff of orange, whiff of smoke. Empty mirror. A ring from a coffee cup last morning. Fingerprint.

Names

First to let go
    of the murderous tongue,
        end of the intimate and divine source
           of the esophagus,
               trained in the schoolbacked
               wooden chair of youth,
               ruler whack of pronunciation
                       shoulder-tossed
                          shout by brotherboys and
                             cousins,
                   this mutation,
    the final journey, arrives in the first melting
where no memorized faces survive.

Then, take out the treasure and bury it below the ice. Perhaps, in a land beyond
memory, it will resurface.

Roll Call

exploding milk carton
bookbag monster eating up filling up the peagreen bus seat space
group history project of one
chingchong
Andy Jackson stealing her bag, contents upchucking over chair, under desk and
        everybody laughing
Jenny Chan's favorite word *fob*
thick rain and mud deposits sliding onto the ugly granite steps
head craning to the mirror of linoleum
dirty bus exhaust greeting and the skyhorizon still flushing pink

Xiaomei's tiny voice asks her mother,

        Why did you bring me here?

Ching Chong
a haibun

Ching Chong Chinaman sitting on a fence Trying to make a dollar out of fifteen-cents Along came a choo-choo train Knocked him in the cuckoo-brain And that was the end of the fifteen cents Ching Chong Chinaman sitting on a wall Along came a white man And chopped his head off Ching Chong Chinaman sitting on the grass Along came a bumblebee and stung him on his Ask no questions tell no lies I saw a policeman doing up his Flies are a nuisance Bugs are even worse And this is the end of my silly little verse Chinky Chinky Charlie went to milk a cow Chinky Chinky Charlie didn't know how Chinky Chinky Charlie pulled the wrong tit Chinky Chinky Charlie got covered in shit Chin Chin Chinaman bought a little shop And all he sold was peppermint rock He wee'd in a bottle and called it pop Chin Chin Chinaman bought a little shop Ching Chong Oh Mister Ching Chong You are the king of Chinatown Ching Chong I love your sing-song When you have turned the lights all down;

four-square concrete patch,
a coven of ruling girls
stomp the sticky seed.

fob 1. to trick or put off (a person) with second-rate articles, lies, excuses, etc. I knew it was a bad word by the way Jenny hurled it, hitting me full in the face. Mrs. Washington wouldn't look at me. Instead, she ordered me to look it up. I told her it meant: a small pocket in the front of a pair of trousers, for carrying a watch, etc; watch pocket; or a short ribbon or chain attached to a watch and hanging out of such a pocket. She couldn't prove me wrong. It said so on p. 547. **2.** to get rid of (something worthless) by deceit or trickery; palm off. Kathy with the red ribbon whose back was my landscape every morning said hello to me in Mr. Hall's class. She asked me many questions, the word for 'hello,' how to say 'pretty,' 'egg,' 'duck,' 'good morning.' Kathy did not talk to me if Courtney, Amanda, Jenny, and Keisha; if Arthur, Jeff, Winston. I told her 'ugly' for 'pretty,' 'quail' for 'duck,' 'shut up' instead of 'good morning.' I told her that her Chinese name was ku li. **3.** free on board **4.** foreign body

Ku Li

cool Li?
Coolly
Coo/glee
Cooled ghee
Chew me
Cruelty
Gruel, tea
Cowrie
Cold feet
Coolie

COOLIE: A HISTORY REPORT

The coolies
were
workers
from
China
who
came
a
long
time
ago.
Here.
They
could
be
my
grandpa's
grandpa's
age.

They
built the
railroad, but

couldn't
go
to

the
party.
They
were
sad
and
mad.

GINGER SOUP

Ma,
did you also love
those wild days,

the morning released after the first gush of winter—

the world soft snow as
the day I

tucked it against my cheek,
perched atop that metal shield of trashcan
flying towards
your hands stirring honey
in the waiting pot?

COOL LI?: *a riddle*

What an unlikely girl, an angle. What strange eyes, the calm bearer of sunglasses. What a bolt, what a length, what an un-turning ear, what a dashed, word-dry mouth. She's nearly a boy, what a fine mess! What this does to the girls all aflutter, how dark the night like caramel when biting into its flanks. And what an unlikely laborer, the hands work steadily through the lunch bells, never minding the hidden eyes, the mouth will come, the hand the only ear. How narrow the house where Xiaomei discovers light.

Xiaomei & Andy

7/8's of the day = bell ringing = carries her to him,
a spiky-haired, leanface Andy
                            diagonal across
                                        aisle.

Hey! #8?, his question a projectile to the headback—
                            Hey, didya hear me, little girl?

One quarter into class, he is still staring.

You can't have this, she wants to projectile into his waiting mean-eyed face.
1/8th remaining = up go the papers to the front.

In the rush, Andy copies furiously, her paper a deception.

I have a long memory, the blue eye hisses.

So do I, boy, so do I.

CRUELTY: *a riddle*

So you think I'm going to write about my mother in her kitchen, delicate love and the family meal. Here in my banished heart, there are no mothers or kitchens.

COLD FEET: *a riddle*

Li leans back
bone straight   *against*   *the spine of locker*
                                                    Xiaomei's only private corner

            two girls inherit the almond eyes of their mothers

Li smiles   the other in the background
the popular girl   with her wistful smile
color slightly off   knows they could be
but still a golden girl   some kind of family
    with flying hazel eyes

Li crooks her arm, beckoning, friendly, a cool breeze of tousled hair.

                Xiaomei

                                                        out of
                                            angles

                                                    breath

                            horse clomping up her
                    vertebrae

                    chomping
                                    collapsing cage

                            blood ribbling
                                knotted grip
                                                    pivot
                                        hell and flees
                                                    down
                                        the stubborn
                                        hallway

                            from her lighter
                    counterpart.

WAKE ME

if i mumble and it's not your name
i know   how names are   precious

                                                                    if there is a dream

there might be

the night   we pulled her from the
shimmering water   and
anger fell straight from her body

how
i wanted
to run in after   her
my body
sliced
to
strips
of
the
most
beautiful skin

The story never stops spinning and I am never used to it.

The True Tale of Xiaomei

This woman with my face   is not mine.
I do not love her   and she does not love me.

Her face would open
     as the ting announced my arrival.

She would sit me down
behind that plank doubling as counter,
     the Sharpie my weapon to nail her tongue onto placard.

I look her in the fierce eye and say,
     No, that's wrong.
     You are not saying it right.

She would halt her recitation,
press her thin peach lips,
     like she was glad I was worth something.

Other twilights, I said nothing,
     daring her to hang her failures in the window.

At school the next day, the girls would gather 'round and I would unfold
The Great Outlandish True Tale of my pathetic mother,
     married off at age three,
     to an evil rich man as second wife/concubine.
     How she squeezed sorrow out of her pounding chest.
     How he beat her for that first daughter (me!).
     How she squirreled away like the workday ant, coin after morsel.
     How one day the bus driver saw my fresh face and her haggard one,
       two sides of the mirror of time   open onto his pale life.
          He fell in love with such courage.

     We a lovely family bought passage on the steerage section of the airplane,
     here to start a romantic,
     rose-tinted life,
     that classic immigrant story that breaks their little Pilgrim hearts
     and who could say otherwise—

                    my mirror of a face ensconced behind
                         a battling cash register waiting
                                for the munchies of college students
                                   or financial district secretaries
                                      on lunch break.

This face,
I the only authority:
translator,
writer,
communicant,
sage,
storyteller,
shit-talker.

How would you,
o foreigner,
know the difference?

How do you not know I am not secretly in love with this face,
which I have never hated,
as you first imagined.
This secret society,
        an imperceptible nod we pass,
            a shit-talking language in which we say nasty things about all the
        foreigners we hate.

Even now, she is carving up her deep memories for me,
        I am scooping out her innards,
                that long imprint of my family before her,
                        hand snaking up what she has stitched shut at the ass.

At the station, the old grandmother,
        mumbling poetic phrases in Mandarin,
a wrinkled-faced woman who could have been my grandmother
presumed I was part of her family.
Filial obligation
would move me to point her
                                in the northern direction towards our tribes.

And that bleak day,
I wanted to talk loudly in another tongue,
shaming her for not knowing my other language,
for marking me with my difference,
a gift from my mother.

But I stuffed myself back into my skin.

She could have missed this smallest turn,
                    sweet opening,
                              but her finger crept up,
                                        touched that nerve,
                                                  and spilled.

Until I picked her up with my split tongue,
          we bartered for those multiple years of bloodshed,
                    empires,
                              emperors,
                                        mandates,
                                                  for our shared failings as daughters,

                                        perhaps not businesswomen who could
                              lift up an oppressed family with one finger,
                                        we stood parked
                    in front of that multi-hued subway map
          at the mouth of the entranceway,
that immigrant port city of all the world.

Never having a lover with my own family face,
I headed home to empty bed.
I cried for all the erasures within myself,
for the sand I had thrown on my mother's memory,
for my hard back.

To love your own violent histories,
the remembered soup of your failings,
and to forgive those who have failed before you,

generation upon generation,
        of the most mad,
            the most terrible,
                  the deadliest secrets crossing the ocean.
We do not bury our dead, but hack them into shanks we lay on our backs,
                  bearing them forever into each new world.

I mention this because   this woman with my face is meeting her end.
I am still the translator,   her fate within the shallow breaths of my hands.
Her eyes ask me to tell her the honest brutality, the fate which only I can deliver.

Again and again,   I am her murderer.

I have been training all my life to place each word in front plainly:
Not to say without saying,
as is the tradition of my family,
or my tribe,
or my country,
or my people.

To love this only woman with my face.

IV

Onion Dreams

A girl, a blossom,
the black fan of hair falling,
what luck to catch her!

—Albert Toke, *Silkgirl*

The Geisha Author Interviews

1. *So, Albert, first of all, why geishas?* *It has nothing to do with geisha in Kyoto.* We probably project our fantasies in the West. There is a certain—exotic world. One of the things that make geisha so curious for us is that if you were to see one perform a dance, you'd find it very exotic and strange. *It has nothing to do with geisha in Kyoto. It has nothing to do with geisha in Kyoto.* The story is he entered my space, hooked me up like a struggling fish. *It has nothing to do with geisha in Kyoto. It has nothing to do with geisha in Kyoto. It has nothing to do with geisha in Kyoto. It has*

Their makeup is pretty nutty-looking. *Very rude Very rude Very rude Very rude Very rude* He claimed he spoke Mandarin, but so poorly, *Very rude Very rude Very rude*

In this culture we really don't have anything that corresponds to geisha so there is a certain exoticism. *The world of geisha is our culture. The world of geisha is our culture. The world of geisha is our culture. The world of geisha is our culture.* I guessed the words like a jigsaw puzzle, stifling my laughter because I didn't want to hurt his feelings. In truth,

2. *So you find geishas exotic?* I was fascinated by the glowing white light of his face, **Alluring to the imagination. See, I was a little kid running around in my bathing suit, and President Truman, actually Harry, he came and had tea while I played with his grandchildren at the pool.** trying out the Great White Whale, see?

3. *So what you're saying is that you had the genes and means?* Story is he brings **Let's just say that I wasn't going to starve to death if my novel didn't sell well. Having grown up on the edge of an empire myself, I was fascinated by illegitimacy. What I mean to say—when I met the son of an industrialist and a geisha, a bastard son, I was in love with his bastardness, never having been a bastard myself, you see?** all his dates to that quiet teahouse but won't tell them we discovered it together.

4. ***So you bastardized the story?*** Sick of that yuppie fusion teabar, I demanded a new
No storyteller or journalist is ever exact enough to please an expert. It's worth
bearing in mind that Hamlet makes poor Danish history and Lawrence of Arabia
grossly oversimplifies the politics and culture of the Middle East.

The first time, I got absolutely everything wrong. *Yes, that is true. Yes, that is true. Yes,
that is true.* experience, which we found in the phonebook. *Yes, that is true. Yes, that*

5. ***When did you begin to realize?*** *is true.* First, when I met my geisha. I had
no idea what I was doing. I had never written fiction before. In college, I stud-
ied Japanese art history, ended up getting a master's degree in Japanese history
and went to live in Japan. I had done a lot of research, but I didn't know how
to enter the world of geisha. *I opened the geisha world for him.* We traveled three
times to the quiet teahouse before we found it open. *I opened the geisha world for
him. I opened the geisha world for*

I filled in the blank spaces with guesses, wrote a draft based on a lot of book-learn-
ing. *On the condition that he would not use my name or my family's name in the book.*
Over a pot of oolong, he described his project, what I secretly nicknamed the Great
White Novel. He was writing about geishas. *On the condition that he would not use my*

Writing geisha was like waging war. Sometimes I felt myself a General charging
forth with strategic decisions. *He broke every promise. He broke every promise. He
broke every promise.* Story? *He broke every promise. He broke every promise. He broke*

Or the guy in the trenches with the rifle.

Once, I lost my muse. There's only so much of the Great Exotic Other you can take.
*"If I should lose my wife, I would live only one year to leave a collection of sad and
beautiful poems behind."—poet Tamiki Hara* Another version involves a woman.

6. *Was she a geisha?* According to whomever you believe, one person left the other, She served the part, although part of being a geisha is not to talk about it. What I really wanted to know was what it was like to be her. Where do you sleep? What do you eat? How do you have your hair done? And she was quite willing.

7. *So help us understand. What is it like to be a geisha, in your own expert opinion?* stranded on an island of their own tears The truth is she doesn't exist. Geisha's entirely invented, and the woman that I interviewed wouldn't recognize herself, or really anything about herself, in my book, which she hasn't read, because she doesn't read English.

8. *What was it like to invent geisha?* *Do you know what shame means to a Japanese?* I remember at one point in the midst of writing it, we went on a tour of the White House. There in the corner was a guard with a little badge and uniform, and I remember having a tremendous sense of envy. This guy had a clear role in the world and everyone knew who he was. And here I was in my little study trying to write this thing and no one knew what I was doing. To me, I was risking my life and I was terrified. *Unless we atone for it in life, it stays with us in death. My eternity, he risked.* & all the tea in the world could not revive them.

Two Truths & A Lie

The story is he entered my space, hooked me up like a struggling fish. He claimed he spoke Mandarin, but so poorly, I guessed the words like a jigsaw puzzle, stifling my laughter because I didn't want to hurt his feelings. In truth, I was fascinated by the glowing white light of his face, trying out the Great White Whale, see?

Story is he brings all his dates to that quiet teahouse, but won't tell them we discovered it together. Sick of that yuppie fusion teabar, I had demanded a new experience, which we found in the phonebook. We traveled three times to the quiet teahouse before we found it open. Over a pot of oolong, he described his project, what I secretly nicknamed the Great White Novel. He was writing about geishas.

Story? There's only so much of the Great Exotic Other you can take. Another version involves a woman. According to whomever you believe, one person left the other, stranded on an island of their own tears & all the tea in the world could not revive them.

TWO RIVER GIRLS

a pantoum

Once there was a river glistening from your hair.
We blessed the glowing candles,
set them in the black water,
waited for a response from the gods.

We blessed the glowing candles.
I kissed your glorious mouth,
waited for a response from the gods,
hoping the beauty of our sins would be enough.

I kissed your glorious mouth,
two girls descended from salt merchants by the sea,
hoping the beauty of our sins would be enough.
We could finally travel that backwards path.

Two girls descended from salt merchants by the sea,
the water rising from what was sacred.
We could finally travel that backwards path,
the stars listening to the songs of the gods,

the water rising from what was sacred.
I am kissing a new body into flesh,
the stars listening to the songs of the gods.
There will be no mischief tonight.

I am kissing a new body into flesh.
What is beautiful can be resurrected.
There will be no mischief tonight,
only the honey between our mouths.

What is beautiful can be resurrected.
Set in the black water,
only the honey between our mouths,
where once there was a river glistening from your hair.

This the story of a boy whose eyes alight on a golden-eyed storyteller . . .

—Dante Johnson, *Spoken Word City*

Two Disciples of the Word

Dante Johnson waits at the curve where sidewalk meets bus.

                           Black corkscrews, brown-edged eyes,
sad creases in his palms like wood etched by a fickle artist, thrift store threads
kissing the street corner.

                    Dante brings an ivory linen envelope,
                        the house of a poem.

                    Poets must eat other poets,
                surviving by ingesting the elders,
                  murdering their young,
           and erasing all sins they spill onto paper.

My own personal poet versifies *the odd converted garage of a cold room, how we*
      string up the lanterns of our prayers, transforming the dungeon.

                              What I remember
                      of my own tinderbox
                        is not gray carpet,
                but each poet he hustles through
3am ambulance sirens, that 24 hour laundromat where the tired prophesy in the next
    darkened doorstep, past the upstairs slaps of my breaking neighbors,

              each poem perched on the roof of his open eyes.

DANTE'S LAMENT

(from Spoken Word City, Track 13, Dante Johnson Live)

a villanelle

Too much war, woman, who knows who's right?
I can't stay, I'm close to killed.
The real poets come out at night.

Backpedaling into rosy light,
sweetgrain words up the hill.
Too much war, woman, who knows who's right?

I return for you, all contrite,
but your sharp ears are filled—
only real poets come out at night.

It's too much, I can no longer fight,
I'm letting go of this guilt.
Too much war, woman, who knows who's right?

Out of mind, out of sight,
we collapse what's built.
The real poets come out at night.

We'll never again be tight,
we'll never again be grilled.
Too much war, woman, we know what's right.
Only the real poets here tonight.

RELEASE

not as in to break a body so you remain whole, and not to dismiss what is built up, a pile of memory, calcified borders between our limbs. Not the boiling frightful phrases, the loose cannon of jealousy, friction, to pain, to hurt, to lodge discomfort, but to set at liberty, to shake off what we discharge, what violence between two venting bodies objecting to the world around them.

The concept of family had never taken hold of me in this way before.

—Jaden Goldfeld,
The History of Jaden/When Jani Recedes: A Memoir

My Lover, a Half-circle Hanging over the Bed

We've been here before: a blank room in New York City, your unframed late-night dream is missing you in Ann Arbor.

We've been here before: your obsession with Oedipus, mine with Eastern salt.

You say,
>   give me your breast and I will baptize it.

You say,
>   give me your heart and I will bathe it.

I don't say,
>   give me your soul. I would not barter for anything less than your open greedy mouth.

FAMILY
a ghazal

In the breathless city, those who wander could be family.
I too bring my bag of cartilage and common name despite family.

My ample mother—a repressed flood—I phone on Sundays.
What guilty treasures might shame this white family?

I met my country, my love, my river, my sweet.
Late Saturday nights, Sunday coffees, and kites like family.

Drought was over. I, salty and lean; she, a cinnamon apple.
Her sweet menstrual blood in the eggshell sheet, tight like family.

Forgive me, mother, I suckled your orchard dry, perhaps.
But now she and I, Xiaomei and Jani, right like family.

Unfurling

My hair down
each evening,
you unbind those plums from the white cloth
and I anoint them
with my mouth.

PEBBLE

solid cool
smooth love round
light in hand, kept in throat
your question about these flying letters
uneasy pebble lodging between two lovers
the first bewildering honeymoon dent
each finger flashlight found the malignant
a sticky ooze of encrusted silence
an irritant we hope pearl
we hope pearl

FAMILY PORTRAIT: XIAOMEI & JANI

a crown of sevens

She's just a good friend to me.
What we share can't be described.

What we share can't be described—
two best friends cooking up dream.

Two best friends cooking up dream—
love's little secret corner.

She's just a good friend to me.

T

To open, to follow, to mirror, to face, to bind (chest), to examine, to pull over (shirt), to button, to spiral, to cook an egg, to toast, to counsel (confusion), to visit (mom), to back (shit), to chicken (out), to (buck) assign, to live, to pass (out), to fist, to girlfriend (early) to come (out) (you'll always be) mine

Letters Found in a Wastebasket

Jani I'd like to talk *Jaden Jaden Jaden Jaden Jaden Jaden Jaden Jaden Jaden Jaden J*
Jani Jani to you girls were always *Jaden Jaden Jaden Jaden Jaden Jaden Jaden Jaden Jad*
Jani Jani Jani girls nothing will *Jaden Jaden Jaden Jaden Jaden Jaden Jaden Jaden Jaden J*
Jani Jani Jani Jani ever change this except *Jaden Jaden Jaden Jaden Jaden Jaden Jaden J*
Jani Jani Jani Jani Jani change *Jaden Jaden Jaden Jaden Jaden Jaden Jaden Jaden Jaden Ja*
Jani Jani Jani Jani Jani Jani I understand boys *Jaden Jaden Jaden Jaden Jaden Jaden Jad*
Jani Jani Jani Jani Jani Jani Jani were always boys *Jaden Jaden Jaden Jaden Jaden Jaden*
Jani Jani Jani Jani Jani Jani Jani Jani getting used to happy *Jaden Jaden Jaden Jaden Jad*
Jani Jani Jani Jani Jani Jani Jani Jani Jani I am asking from you some *Jaden Jaden Jade*
Jani Jani Jani Jani Jani Jani Jani Jani Jani Jani things you may never understand *Jaden*
Jani Jani Jani Jani Jani Jani Jani Jani Jani Jani Jani any questions you may what *Jaden*
Jani Jani Jani Jani close to someone when you are always hiding *Jaden Jaden Jaden J*
Jani Jani Jani Jani Jani Jani Jani something I have been intensely *Jaden Jaden Jaden Ja*
Jani Jani Jani Jani exploring who I am reminder if you slip *Jaden Jaden Jaden Jaden Ja*
up I can't do it any *Jaden Jaden Jaden Jade*

intend to begin living full-time as a man *Jaden Jaden Jaden Jaden Jaden*
I only ask that you begin to use male pronouns I can't do it any longer I am still
the same person, though I worry I will lose I want who I am on the inside to
match what I see on the outside I'm struggling I know this is the right thing for
me

Xiaomei's Zuihitsu for Shapeshifters

1. I watch what you collect at the doorstep of your younger days—the sharp slash of cheek, the shriveled breath clench, a knuckle mid-flight searching for the wooden melody of door, the ghost girl sliced above your shoulders to short shreds of hair.

2. Those shared-blanketed nights you teased me about my sharp, upturned shoulder, a dreaming javelin launched too high.

3. Before burning down the nightlight, unravel the day's slights, the gleam of what we do not fear, what is left without the weight of thread.

4. Sleeping means to settle with the threads of your new chosen name into the traffic of our bed.

5. A letter written halfway seven times, then a waterlogged phone call after a brown winter. Your silver mother, a sheath in the cut door.

6. Gargle of words, cut eyes, a popped balloon.

7. I am the kernel, the diseased molecule when your mother calls.

8. What uneasy collects in the cold chest. What thin lung. What sliced bone. What colored blood.

9. What's love got to do with it?

10. Love, stay just a lil' bit longer. I open the window of my bed, a crawlspace for air.

11. A mother's love is (not) unconditional.

12. A condition—no mothers or foreign girlfriends. No name change. No difference.

13. No phone calls.

14. Where we danced, next to the glowing midnight ledge, the candlelight drifting like a butterfly in my hair, the black gravel of your voice calling, calling home.

Re/Naming/The Other

Let me release *tossed out mutant tossed mutant*   *Let me uncover* tossed out mutant
the murder feelings *tossed out mutant tossed m*   *the killing tongue* utant out tossed
knifecut bled and let out *tossed out mutant tos*   *the deep wound path* sed out mu
my pale unwrapped throat *tant tossed out mut*   *against your unforgiving history*
what I learned combat *ant tossed out mutant to*   *I wear my schooling on my skin*
not in my jacket of choice *ssed mutant tossed o*   *and this is my costume* ut mutant
whipped to girlish frequency *tossed out mutan*   *my tongue unnatural* t tossed out

tossed out mutant *tossed out* mutant *tossed out* mutant *tossed out* mutant *tossed out*
mutant tossed out *mutant* tossed out *mutant* tossed out *mutant* tossed out *mutant*

My final journey arrives   *when I have chosen*
in the melting flesh   *in my quilted dialect*
pared down   *my own name*
to the boy I am   *and you remember this*

BLAME
a crown of sevens

everything and my mother,
hairy pot, clang clang tea and
hairy pot, clang clang tea and
you mold and shower remain
you mold and shower remain
I trail you disrupt letter,
everything and my mother.

SEPARATING

You request my presence.

I agree,
as expected.

Neither of us look forward.

Only this hospital bed,
two numbed bodies,
one hand reaching down to touch its
old friend,
     a bit of comfort before the flesh
                swept away.

We meet in the dull morning.

In a few days,
we will both walk out of this small city.
You, a new man.
Me, a liberated woman.

Burning Down the House

1.

Because this engorged fire-flesh
must begin in a room like this,

3. I was   *a square room where I buried my cowrie*
a child   *among the artifacts*
of the corner
living between   *or, two streets over,*
my desk   *over a scratched oak table and the memory of drowned cups,*
of   *the battle with the trickster word,*
books   *I spell six letters—*
and   *k   n   i   g   h   t*
my   *cah-nah-ai-guh-huh-tuh*
rooms   *into laughter,*
of misspellings   *Mrs. W. shakes no,*
                eyes alight on the next beating body,

The institution   *or, the stubbled street my mother pulled past to the boxed ancient hallway,*
of book lending   *a ruby throat opening to lined shelves,*
opened up   *slanted spines like stacks of spider hulks,*
like a throat   *a fat carmine house pressed against a dwarf stub.*
of a whale

                She drew me to the center,
                  pressed hard on my shoulder
                where the answer should lodge.

Each book each brick   *In the house of sunset paper,*
rested upon the grave   *lived a shining boy answering each distress,*
of another   *each alarming fire chortling through the deserts and the oceans,*
a borrowed hero   *disrupting his own story to enter back to my room*
lived in the house *with the borrowed corner and buried cowrie,*
of rusty pages
no fault   *where I sound you correctly over and over,*
little   *your name attending to the steaming of the rice,*
blame   *before the sweetfleshsun hangs up her hat against the crook of the moon,*
before night kidnaps the lovely sun and drags her away in bound anklets.

2.
In the flush of the room's breathing muscle,
I glance a sweet glimmer of that red-book knight
in the girl across the room,
the corner of that peach mouth curved like flashing tail,
could only stare at that curving hook when she smiled,
which in the retelling became when you gloried at me.

You kissed me on the same rubbled street,
I excavated you from the heavy book,
my coiled mass unwrapping into one easy breath.

Though we live in alternate beds,
having shed each other like a flock of new bodies,
this blood traveling between us,
now a greased-down thin trail we tug,
deep in our segregated nights.

Today, the wind is churning and upset.
Today, the sky is remaking itself over and over.
Today, I am the realization that saying please forgive me is not that difficult.
I am the realization that I am still practicing.
I am the realization that my Chinese name was a gift, not a burden.
I am in the space between fury and exhilaration.
I am in the space between I release and I love.
I am shedding my body for you.
I am writing more letters.
I am releasing my guilty words.
I am releasing my self-criticisms.
I am releasing my high school.
I love what is possible when you crack open and ask.
I love the moment of exhale on Sundays before the week attacks.
I love the communal activity of making soup.
I love working with the grandmas, how they bring me sweet treats and cluck over me.
I love uncovering family history.
I love.

—Jing Jing Chan,
declarations in a letter to Xiaomei

A Letter From My Former Mortal Enemy

Dear Xiaomei,

You wonder why you hold a burning white leaf in your hands and where it has come from.

A fair question, there are no neutral words.
But no hidden spiders belong in the package.

Did you know they called us sisters? When I said no, they said cousins. Then, lezzies who no boy would kiss. I hated you, your thighhigh mintgreen socks, your bushy braid trailing down your rigid back, your tin pencil case, your shell-less voice.

I, a metal scrap, was not willing to be your road.

I wish I could cradle those two little girls, two cramped onions we were, and lift them out to the opening world.

What I am trying to say is, I'm sorry.

Sincerely,

   Jing Jing (Jenny) Chan

LETTER TO THE FORMER BULLY

Dear Jing Jing,

I have started my reply back to you seven times,
but found myself dry in the gulf of what I meant to write.

What I've learned about moving—

      the world unsheathes the body,
            the tellers roam and find
                  the story hidden from you,
    only because you weren't listening
                      in the right key.

      Xiaomei

CHEW ME: *a riddle*

Then a key falling through the dreams of each girl, each letter a crescendo, an urgent lifting, a scab finally taking breath, the tender kiss of epidermis and sky—

then Jing Jing writes—

> *nobody gave him to us,*
> *but we dug our hands deep and worked the flesh of our paper-son,*
> *crooned to him until we recalled:*

>> *eight crooked steps upon which the journey rested—*

>>> *the first, the entrance to a cave where a red maiden hid from the jealous winter sun;*

>>> *the second, the love seat of the butcher, which we believed, having seen the entrails of a boar encrusted on the stone;*

>>> *the third where my uncles were shot;*

>>> *the fourth never existing because of terrible luck;*

>>> *the fifth, a wedding present;*

>>> *the sixth, inlaid with glitter from the West, brought by the smooth-talking salesman of flesh who visited the summer before he left;*

>>> *the seventh, a stoop used for writing letters, such as those sent across the sea;*

>>> *the eighth, a question mark;*

>>> *because, of course,*
>>>> *these steps never belonged to my own blood family,*
>>>> *but cramped together in the red book my great-great-great-great-grandfather purchased in the pursuit of the golden sun,*
>>>> *these eight stone slabs the secrets of his new bought*
>>>> *family inked into that red book he ate during that crossing;*

*although he did not anticipate that the foreigners would
keep him hemmed in at the edge of the Western hemisphere
with a gang of cursing men who had been sold the same
song by smiling salesmen and who passed their days shit-
talking in rhyme into the grooves of the wood wall for fear
of tattling.*

Years later,
    I had to go see for myself.
    I scooped tourist ice cream,
    collected envelopes from the aunties,
    charged the rest of my plane ticket,
    and boarded the ferry to Angel Island and treaded through those
        bereft rooms,
    hoping for a voice to speak.
    None did,
    so I crept into my ancestor,
    stole his breath for a poem
    I placed in his mouth like a prayer—

                The West stole the dragon's heart,
                I came to claim dignity;
                out of water, the ants play,
                but still the dragon will live—

    and wore those words back home
    to my people since
    who would disbelieve me,
    so now we have a secret
    between us,
    like blood sisters.

Lightning Love
a zuihitsu

1

Possible actions when dealing with living ghosts—

a phone call   with white space,
an arrangement,
a chat awkwardly,
a rendez-vous.

I choose all of the above.

2

Silver, the collected color of making amends—a cool flash of grumbled lightning fled down each throat, sweet mercury.

3

Glancing sideways in mirrors, she could be me. Dreaming of pleasure, I glide my hand into the lagoon, like only I know how.

4

The neighborhood coffeeshop, the rippling guitar and bass, the curved black tarnish of the seat revealed when she vanishes to the candle-scented bathroom, the same thin spindle pressed chill against my hard skin, the yellow flame of lantern chained to the pipe overhead, the still overhead fan.

5

My water is not flashing hot or steel cold. She appreciates the extremes of her water.

6

Her pupils—black magnets—shine with the hidden sweet rabbit on the moon. Sit for me, I beg her, the perfect subject, as the reflection in her eyes beckons.

7

A pilgrimage to our shared table, a half-roasted sandwich, a bitter coffee, a journal, a sour dream, a cleansing shit before the next greeting.

8

A woman's worth is not built from love.

9

Xiaomei's bellybutton, a whirlpool in a honey pancake.

10

Two curled for heat, two melting milk chocolate bars sweat and sweet.

11

I place two spoons next to the mud-baked bowls of gruel. I learned this from my mother who can no longer eat anything except sweet water. I leave Xiaomei an S in my bed.

DIALECT

bright shocking talismen blinking smog windows ice cream factory ginger girls
dying weeds compressed in red ornamental silk plastic fried menu gold gaud ani-
mal discharge golden tofu stink smoking boys by gray fruit peeling river dirty-
white-smock man giving you lonely eye fisheye steaming silver cart with 10,000-
feet smell the tall the pale with laminated Lonely Planet maps the mouths the
flapping mouths

—ascension into that airless hole

pass
stinklockers
pass
multi picket lingual signs
pass
autoansweringmessage
pass
furred gray women at coffee hour with neon worker compensation flyers
pass
weightlifting manuals
pass
home of the living mice and the tailor's nest
drain drain drain
the janitor and the bullhorns in storage
the dust the dust the dusthawkers

how your lips open in flight

Coo/Glee: *a riddle*

To divide beauty from the sky,
eleven borrowed words
breed in the still space.
In this fistful of kisses,

a silver mirror,
the water's reflection,
a woman's bellybutton,
two spoons.

MIDNIGHT TERRAIN

Here is the workman leather of your sole,
here is the shining grape, the toe,
here the leg,
the knee, the mountain,
slippery upper gorge,
here the holder of the belly, sweetlined center radiating all juice,
breast, thick and heavy, spigot and arch,
underbelly of chin here,
the North, the South of your face,
your rumbling lip,
half-mast

nose,
starving ears,
the high bones,
the wall, built-up chain of the eye,
     only visible window,

       and what I harvest—

   that horse, that snail, that thousand inner mouths chewing on my dust,
     how you hold me in and crumple,
       the blood shoveling through the pipes,
         the bursting bursting moan of teakettle.

Lost Poem #8

one. we are the people. two. a lil' bit louder. three. we want justice. four. the third world. One!

We Are The People! In the beginning were the students. The students came into the world because. Their mothers and fathers were in the world in front of them and they got in line. There were many things to do. They made the signs from the blood in the paint can. They dialed the numbers of the helpful bureaucrats. They signed the damn contracts. They hid. They faxed the document. They practiced. They grouped. They did not love anything. What I mean is, there were priorities and there was letting go. There was labor and there was money and they were not the same thing. *Two!*

A Lil' Bit Louder! Though you are just a picker your nature is to gather you are gathering a loudspeaker you are just supposed to be a box on wheels that is what you signed up for you just want the box on wheels which should be pedaled by the hippie the next day march in the midst of the funneling of what you mean to say into a different format it is too early now for peddling he wants something from you you are more than just a human cargo early morning some body is standing between you and the innocent loudspeaker blocking the light raining from the sunrise but not the sound of the warblers how could you move you do not. *Three!*

We Want Justice! What can I tell you that you don't already know? What we want often kills us. *Four!*

The Third World! This street in transition has dreamed of emptying its cargo for years. It has had enough of the hobos and we. It fills with old cooks and old carpenters delivering their daughters to school at first light. What the seamstress has by the hand, it could not be hope in the bare flesh.

Xiaomei's Biography of Sparrow

In the morning, I rush to set down what has blazed over me in the night—
the tiny feasts, the sliding hands, how she's turning towards—
and how would it feel to put my hand there—
in the doorway—
to have been the mud curling at the toes
them there
my tongue,
if I had said,
please.

GOLDFRUIT

"The problem here is that this isn't pretty, the sort of thing which can be easily dealt with with words."
—Cornelius Eady

"Now I just want a grapefruit. I'm leaving you with the apple," Xiaomei says when I enter with moonwhite slices.

I don't want any, but apply my mouth with duty, sipping pale liquid.

Last week in Chinatown, we almost bought a papaya—burntsun wrinkled spots, starpucker ass and all.

Broken thumbprint on lizardcool skin. Pause.

Look again—snout widening, base of a stout neck supporting pulp and seed of a fragrant but barren cranium.

To bring home already bruised fruit, faded freckles, warrior markings, transgressive footsteps?

We decided against it.

I offer a slightly lopsided grapefruit to the desk surface, her pen scratching, thick black dents raining on silent page.

I leave her, slip into unwashed summer sheets, dreaming cool bamboo mats.

Morning, uneaten grapefruit greets, a crescent of a surprise, sunrise.

You Dead Will Never Return

a wryneck

Because I wanted to say yes a thousand times
stars roped into our argument.

Because you lost your way down
that dank path over knotted roots into the loving water.

Because I remained counting my own stars on that cold
riverbank with a thousand searching firefly lanterns.

Because you rose a lilyghost from the lakewater of my dream.

Because I've loved a thousand
men to forget the flush of your matching braids.

Because I, too, battled the churning water,
did not dare think of your bones in your dirt.

Because my feet sank down finally on the rough
ground, my mouth still counting breath.

Because you dead will never return.

WE DON'T KNOW HOW TO LOVE EACH OTHER

We walk on, hands together,
awkward crabs scuttling in a New England church.
Already, you are leading and I am
struggling to match the steady stride.
Already, I am in that night's dream,

                          fingers lifting

                                            out

        of the ground.

        You are not there.

Here, your almond-scented tips trace the corners of my expectant mouth.

3. Girl   I milk the sap. I brew the ailing tea. I boil.   I secret my girl. I pocket my bitter
vegetable, like my cheek. I spark   I rim I glow I fire   Ants walk up and
down my spine. What if digestion? I am of the frozen.

1. The Writer   I am empty of all motion.   2. The Organizer   I burndown to wind.

Secret—my skin peat hides under the   Today, we are a marshmallow before
Covers. Thunder god, a grandfather,   the alarm.   There are no chairs in
Both blisters. A bit apple fed to the   Today, I am the waking sky, composing
Monster who feeds. What makes an   my   a sandwich. house.
Elephant? Thank hunger, make the   Today, I am an ant making room.
Bread. Three is what steals and binds,   In my house, there are 10,000 books in a shrine. No
What compounds in the coffee.   pens   I am liquid and tilting books.   because we are
poor. The official visits me; I am national   I am the realization that saying yes to
    It has less to do with me than   A doesn't mean saying no to M.
You.   treasure and have to prove it.   I am creating the feeling of drinking tea
        What myth is made of: if only if only if   at any time of the day.   lantern.
    What is sacred is mine in my   Then the translators pawn their wedding jewelry for
Cup.   pronunciation class, plunk down into   I am creating myself with shorn   pilots, come
to come feed. They bring notebook, they ask question.   rivertide at the shoulder.
They write and write and say hmmm   I am releasing my unreasonable fear of
amongst themself. There is no water. They say ok, they liquid bodies. buy Pepsi.
            I am releasing the owner of the land.
They cannot stomach what is. There is no key. There is no key.   There is no key.
Milk the sap. Brew the ailing tea.   I am releasing the packed train car and
        Pocket the bitter   how we cattle each other into
vegetable, like the cheek. Boil. Secret the girl.   spiderwebs.
Spark. Rim Glow Fire. Ants walk up   I am releasing the grainy mayor. and
down the spine.   I am releasing the stranger who thinks
What if digestion? Of the frozen. Empty all motion.   we're the same girl because.
        Burn down to wind.
            I love that girl who still sleeps when I
        No.   clang the door to the world shut.
            I love saying good night to the cook
                shooting straight from the F
                train in the dawn.
            I love saying no to the pile as an
                empowered worker.

I love pork and salty fish Fridays.
I love that no one took credit, the rally
	organized itself in the horizon
	between the metal door
	and the street.
I love how Auntie Joan has no cell
	phone and all the other women's
	phone numbers on speed dial in
	her head.

I love that Xiaofeng's dream is of a blue
	house near blue grass rising from
	a steaming valley.

BLACK LIGHT

1.
A hammock, teacups and
a shiny piano. Coffee grinds grow
in the spaces they have not
commandeered in the sink.

2.
She holds her breath
as if you live here.
Your breasts, she cannot stop looking.
Your voice flowing from the sky, like cold rain.
She doesn't want
your dissolving face
in her fear,
until the night buries feet in the bed,
until she demands that the door shut.

3.
They are territories of skin, desert.
Furred insects lengthen in
their dreams.
No collapsing house.

Yet fester is an unborn child—
they cook it in the soup
and try to divide their portions.

SOME MOTHERS

are like ours:
always

writing their elegies:
and yet,

we would harvest those slivers of fantasy
when they were all we held onto:

those planks of salt,
those filled dishes.

there is deep
separation in living:

Your living mother
and my dead one.

FEEDING THE WATER
a bop

River between us grows solid
monsters and red meat
compost sludge sneering
the rain I dream unending
water top layer oil and dark
bobbing heads

I'm waiting for that final moment
You'll say the words that I can't say

Each ghost owns her own birth story
but death belongs in the open
we burn firewood gold houses
sweet rind she billows
fat I am sick unyielding
haunt can't be chased out with
candlewick bribed with sweetback
pork the seal of red

I'm waiting for that final moment
You'll say the words that I can't say

But two ghosts in one house
unraveling spools of black thread hair
your still face spread against the pillow
maybe exiting dream
or smothering stars
against the airtight window

I'm waiting for that final moment
You'll say the words that I can't say

Fifth Day of Silence

two haibun

1

One early day, a young mother, carefully stowed in the flanks of a ship packed with chains, set out for a voyage like a flea. The mother was crossing to a weary house to be locked up next to the crab-filled waters. Each night after the daily meal of gruel, the expectant mother prayed to the father, wedged between a field and a mountain. The father tasted each prayer like balm, like a blanket to lie down on beside the twisted wooden tracks he kept watch over.

O to my crushed love,
I did not wish to steal you
singing to the spring.

2

It is what it is
The bird sings or it does not
Who knows who you are

Chinatown is half the size it was when you first arrived. It is widely rumored that it will be no more, if we double our years in commitment. Seven days ago, I was without you, looking up at the marble gate blocking a line of cars doing midday battle. Then, at the heavy doors of the cooling red temple, paint flakes. The closet-sized hot dog stand and the Vietnamese market selling subs. I know I cannot expect them to stay, but I want to remember when they are gone, the sounds of commerce dissipating into the breaking sky.

NOTE FROM A GUEST LOVER

"It ruins them eventually, what they can never have again."
—Stephen Dunn

Sparrow is never coming back, and I am leaving.

I took what I wanted – that slippery dress, shiny fishnets, and put the rest in the wash (don't forget to hang them up to dry). My eyes traveled the quicksilver moon last night, while you slept, dreamless as always.

I HOLD AGAINST YOU:

electricity of your lifting foot,
half-turned hip to the salt terrain,
crease of the empty stomach,
bitter shoulder physics,
your elbow is leaving.
This valley in your face
      where a crooked eye resides,
            channel connecting riverfish
            dipping into the wide stream of my face.

After all,
    were we not
    the great children
        of the opportune,
    conspiring in the same boat,
        fish of the slippery graspers.

COOLLY: *a riddle*

I am singing to you from the end of the world. At night during the traveling hours, I ride clouds in search of the wall you sleep under, hoping that my luck will pull me through the correctly chosen door, the artery of your curled body, any opening that can be salvaged without your knowledge.

I wish this to be easy, at the same time, I wish this to be difficult.

Remember that churning furnace we labored between us, hefted on our empty backs, breaking open? I miss those scorpion days, the color red, the fierce papaya, the melting of skin, our singed hair, our baking shoulders half-whipped by the sun. Yet this memoried seed, this fermenting bone, this weapon of myself you hold hostage. Not yours to repent or to cherish.

I am burnt down to the barest nub, rising up with skin grafted from sea-sisters, knees molded to fight these demons.

What We Do

Either Sparrow is dead or she is never coming back.

If Sparrow disappears either she is firefly or not.

If Sparrow became firefly either this is a necessary dream to coat the brick pain or
not.

If Sparrow's firefly nature is dream either we feel responsible or we do not.

If we feel responsible either we will make amends or we will stay quiet.

If amends are to be made either we are clear what who why or we travel to find
out.

If our life shapes around the discovery of atonement either we love again or we
will not.

If we love again either we experiment and learn or we fail.

If we experiment and learn and fail we experiment learn fail.

You Who Never Arrived:

I have already surrendered
enough of these sturdy valves,
phrases of my half heart—

You who never arrived
in the holding pattern
magenta in the other room:

I studied the meaning of empty,
ghostscribbling on a napkin
leaving in its meteor wake.

We learned to hone down our
Violins and laugh our ordinary
ordinary songs into the vacant
night sky.

And what I cannot do
is pretend we were not content.

How Sparrow Became Firefly

a
subtlesilly
smallsweetsettling
no spilled southsky
save spiraling surface startle
non-luminescent street salve sun sly slick
spawning sand source
spoons signal
softspy

somber sap spinfuck swarm
softbody sprawl scheme
spoilt scavenge
strife   suck
sick spoons sick
suitable stop suitor
spears
sunslickstarfight

spinnning
slowly
shortsnowstub
sporous   sow seed
spiralstucksin
specialized slug
snail
springspringsprung sly sun
synchronize
similar sac spontaneous
shadows
stimulate

saliva
of
a sea   lantern
a   short-term

INVENTING THE TIGER

Xiaomei dreams herself a clearing of green,
a gathering of cool stone,
a locking gate.

A girlbirth in the flanks of the zodiac,
a gift of fossilizing heat,
a blood father,
a stoked rage.

An ear of stealth,
breath of flute and cymbal,
fang of ivory,
a black splash,
surprise in a sunrise.

In this amphitheater
awaiting the mass flight of witches,
come those purloined gradeschool words,
the last of the condemned prisoners,
a lover's discarded name,
empty glass bottle for saving,
these old-school magician songs.

What is consigned must be digested thoroughly,
the pulp hung from the frame.

Opening from the fray—

a bruise-haired,
gold-dipped
woman
lifting
into
sea
of
sky.

Notes

Cooled Ghee: *a riddle*	after Terrance Hayes
Some Say	after Joy Harjo
Dear S,	after Sarah Gambito
Names	after Eric Gamalinda
Ku Li	after Harryette Mullen
cool Li?: *a riddle*	after Li-Young Lee
The True Tale of Xiaomei	after Li-Young Lee
Two Truths & A Lie	after Marlon Unas Esguerra
The Geisha Author Interviews	Some of the text based on found interviews with Arthur Golden, author of *Memoirs of A Geisha*, and Mineko Iwasaki, the geisha he used as a model for the book.
My Lover, a Half-circle Hanging over the Bed	after Marlon Unas Esguerra
Re/Naming/The Other	after Tyehimba Jess
We Don't Know How to Love Each Other	after Anna Akhmatova
Some Mothers	after Faiz Ahmed Faiz
Black Light	after Ann Kong
Feeding the Water	Italicized lines from New Order's "Bizarre Love Triangle"
What We Do	after Anne Carson
You Dead Will Never Return	after a nonce form by R.A. Villanueva

Ching-In Chen is a poet and multi-genre, border-crossing writer. She is the daughter of Chinese immigrants and is a Kundiman Asian American Poet Fellow. A community organizer, she has previously worked in the Asian American communities of San Francisco, Oakland, and Boston. Currently, she lives in Riverside, where she is in the MFA program at University of California Riverside.